Chokri

Yorkshire Publishing
TULSA

ISBN: 978-1-960810-05-2
Chokri

Yorkshire Publishing
1425 E 41st Pl
Tulsa, OK 74105
www.YorkshirePublishing.com
918.394.2665

Published in the USA

Chokri

By

Sandra Greenwell and Cassandra Greenwell

Contents

Phase One - Love

Preface

I do not proclaim to be an expert in love,
Its many variations,
Its venom,
I have known enough.

What I do know,
If my experience is true,
Love is not ever expected,
It isn't what we initially view.

Whatever prefaces, previews and promotions we think,
Love is never that,
Its impact and appearance,
Is never what we predict.

So read on,
And see…
Our views of love,
They are our message,
Full and free.

The Lake

Upon the lake there sat two girls,
Both alike in locks with curls.
One a poet, a dreamer of kinds.
One an intellect, a realist in time.

They sat looking out,
Whilst at each other.
Wise as the winds,
Seasonal as the stone.

The ripples may carry them,
To separate banks.
But they do not allow the gentle pull,
Close... They stay.

As the dove does fly true,
The orchard fruitful,
They stay. They stay. They stay.
True, strong, they stayed.

To the Moon and Back

To the moon and back
To the moon and back
I hear people say it often
To the moon and back...

Is it synonymous with love?
No, I dare say not.
Is it a tangible quantity?
Probably. But, I still dare say not.

So … what?
What is the meaning?
Except conformity to the norm.

To the moon and back
Love is the quantity being measured here.
But does it need measuring if it is held dear?

What meaning does it hold,
If it is constantly foretold?
Don't tell me you love me to the moon and back.
I don't believe it.
It means nothing.

Maybe it means something...
I am unsure.

I am unfair.

But in my own heart,
I want someone to say,
Something a little more.

Spark

Potential
Possibility
A pathway, a choice, tempting eyes.

A dark night,
As lips were closer than mere friendship would allow.

Chilling bricks, too frigid on the skin.
But the contact, the touch, it was enough to singe.

Tempting each other,
Friendship is gone here.
What will it become?
We will see over the years.

Teasing their desires,
As they can feel each other's lips tremor.
Holding until one breaks. Sincere agony to not give in.
And they do.

The bonfire lit,
It is ablaze.
As their lips meet
Their bodies engage.

Touching fire, being fully inflamed.
I know the feeling well.
When we stopped being just friends... On that day.

A Note to You

The sparkle is back!
Shining and bright,
Yesterday has gone…
The sadness in flight.

You deserve the best
Be happy my child
Enjoy your life
And make it worthwhile.

My prayer,
Let grace and kindness
Be plentiful in your life,
And bind you with happiness,
My child with your wife.

Hung

She looked at me,
As I lay in my own self-inflicted pain.
Weary and still.
As she doted upon me,
Ensuring my eventual recovery, she asked
"Is there anything I can do for you?"

I looked at her plainly and replied
"Love me, unconditionally, for the rest of our days"
"Ok" was the word that followed.

Camp

In her absence, the mind plays tricks,
Making you feel as though she is there.
All the - while - the realisation…
She is elsewhere.

The touch of her hand
Fingers interlocked with my own
Is the sea and the breeze on a warm summer's day
It is the night's sky unclouded,
Vibrant with the galaxies at play.

To peer into her engulfing brown eyes
Deep with knowledge of all that is wise
With specs of gold and black
Those eyes… I could stare into and never look back.

For being apart for a week
May seem like an insignificant fracture
But it serves to remind the heart, head and soul
That you want her.

Snoring

The snores go on,
They never stop
As you rest your weary head,
A cacophony of blaring sounds,
Symphonies even dreads.

What happens in your mind at night?
I often wonder,
Dear.
What on Earth possesses you,
To make such sounds so queer.

Love – Part 1

Consider love a gift, that has been specially bestowed your way,
Be true to yourself,
Be honest, be kind,
Share your laughter, your tears,
Your uttermost fears,
Victories, defeats,
Even the littlest of feats.

Love needs to be nurtured,
It cannot survive on its own,
It needs care and patience,
Constant attention,
Listen to it carefully,
Don't moan!

Standing in your shoes 41 years ago…
vowing to love, honour, respect,
the words freely flowed…

As years passed by
Their understanding dawned more clearly.
As we challenged this emotion,
Pushing it to its limits, causing commotion
Struggling to understand it,
We persevered – fought…

prepared to give it a go
Realising love is not stagnant
It needs room to breathe and to grow.

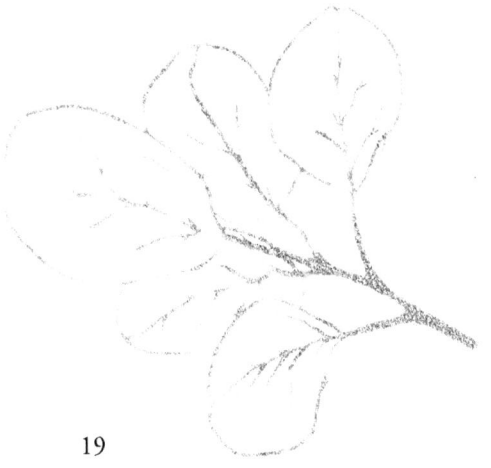

Love – Part 2

Clichés comparing love to a red rose fill my mind.
A word hard to define.

With so many variations on the meaning
The word is hard to pin down
It elusively evades me
Drives me crazy.

Capturing the myriad of emotions
In one word.
Makes you realise that it is not big enough
Not nearly sufficient,
Definitely not efficient.

But what does love actually mean?

Liking, learning, lust, longevity
Openness, oneness, opulence, obsession
Vibrant, vital, vicious,
Euphoric, empathetic, emotional and empowering.

Words can't quite pin it down,
Elusive it is with its smiles and its frowns.

For me it was love when I first held my children…
When they smiled (possible wind),

First words, steps, burps and frowns.
Hangovers, vomiting and all
It had to be love, my heart knew its call.

As the years passed by,
Their love showed me all.

A Note to a Friend

Hollowed out,
We are but flesh and bones,
Exposing our thoughts to another…
There is no greater risk.

When your spirit,
Finds kindred…
I hope it is real.

Understanding the pros of our lives,
The syntax of our verbs,
A rarity, is this…
I dare say.

So if you find,
A soul who knows,
To reply in kind,
Without fake, faltered rows.

They see your eyes,
Read your creases,
They regard your words,
Your thoughts,
Your pieces.

It is not rehearsed,
Love should never be as such.
It is an understanding…

It is in the word,
It is in the look,
It is in the touch.

Phase Two - Loss

Preface

If you live,
As I hope you do
Life, is not all love,
There is loss too.

It can break you,
As it did me.
Encompassed in regret,
Distant.

We learn to suppress,
Managers of our own minds,
We must soldier on,
Left foot, right.

Do not fear loss,
It is part of life.
Keep those close,
Our memories are where they are alive.

Ghosts

Looking down at the stream
A silhouette
Appeared
Slim, tall, almost pretty
Long, flowing hair
A wistful look in the soulful eyes.

A ripple and then it was gone
Disturbed by the water fowl.

Come back, he pleaded
Don't go…don't leave me…
Reaching out to touch the shape
Hoping to feel the soft skin
It was no more – just a ripple…
A wisp of thin mist left in its wake.

The kookaburra mockingly laughed
As he cried out in despair
"Come back"
Tears slowly finding their way to the water
A face full of sadness
Looked back at him.

Persephone

It is the day,
The day of supposed joy
I feel nothing of this.
Nothing...

I miss you,
Deep... It is the core of me.
Longing for us,
Longing for you.

The fresh blooms that follow my arrival,
The decay that accompanies me home,
I miss your smile.

I am condemned,
Rotten, rotting
To walk with Hades forevermore.

Then snapped away for a time, blinked.
With Demeter, my mother, mum...
Oh how I miss you
Oh how I love you
Oh how I remember...

My eyes open again,
Dragged and loaded.
She is gone
And I am a shadow.

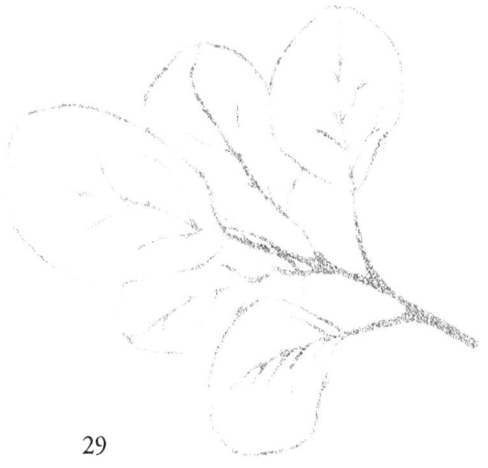

Barbara

On the sixth day, the sixth sister returned,
She came with the sun
She left with the moon.

The stories, oh the stories she told,
Of love, life, laughter
Of tears that her heart wept,
Of times the world would not forget.

The wrinkles worn of a survivor now gone,
Replenished back to the fresh blossom of a newly
bloomed soft petal flower.
She was walking amongst them.

At first... it was confusing.
Where? She wept to no one, to nothing...
She followed the laughter the wind carried on its travels.
She followed it far.

She followed in the footsteps everyone must walk one
day,
Till her eyes met another.
"Birdie?"

An embrace long missed,
From those sisters six,
It does not replace what remains in flesh and bone,
But those six, they feel just like home.

Jono

How long will you stay?
She asked in concern
"The wind did bring me and it will take me back", he replied

The sands hold the story,
For a moment.

The steps fading, quickly, we must get this down.
The thunderous laughter is stirring the clouds.

An imprint in the water, fleeting yet fine,
Is left in my memory for that time.

Chasing the moon away the sun shines too bright,
Will the wind return?

Bike

The girl I saw cycling
was you
Long, honey brown tresses flowing,
flying free.

Your face absorbed the sunshine,
With total abandonment.
You looked serene, happy,
A wild contentment.

My heart leapt with joy and excitement,
Your name caught in my throat.
Turning back, looking again
The image now focussed

The girl I saw cycling,
Looked just like you…
Alas my eyes deceived me
Old age is an impediment.

The girl I saw cycling
Was … I wish
You.

Imperial Leather

As I washed my hands of their dirt and filth,
At a gathering of foggy minds, a scent rose up at me.
It was a forgotten fragrance, no perfume of such.
It reminded me of a flightless bird.

This bird had been stranded,
I never thought it would leave me.
We spent such time together
As she chirped wild stories to me.

The bird, pure, where others were not.
Drinking sweet nectar nightly on the dot,
A ritual.

No, I never did think she would leave this old bird.
Despite being aged,
In my youth I had never experienced true loss.
Only ever heard. But she did. One day.
She took her last flight, up somewhere, mostly away.
Memories are when I see that sweet bird,
I can hold her again.
The hole that was left you will never understand,
Till you lose a bird that was part of your plans.
No more seeing, hearing or bonding to be shared.
Left with the memories and a hole, paired.

It does get easier, as now I have aged.
My mind wonders beyond that old bird and her gaze.
But that scent, Imperial Leather… Brought her back.
For a moment that bird was chirping at me once again
and I could chirp back.

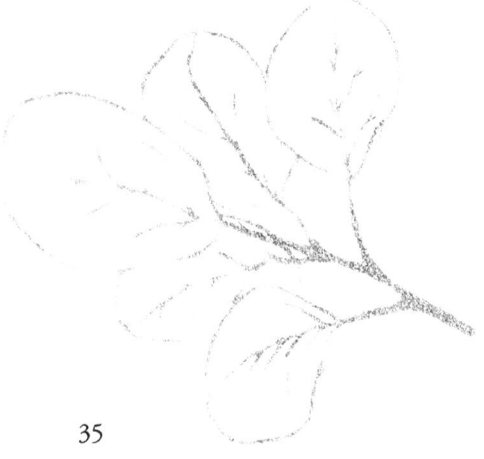

The Nest

As she flew back,
To her newly made nest,
To her newly made life,
To her newly made rest,

A stirring in the stomach occurred,
It tormented, it turned
It wrenched as it wrecked,
Racking the insides with an initially dull blade.

Not remaining so...
Time sharpened the senses
It sharpened the touch
It sharpened the time.

That time had slipped,
The bird's littlest bird had now grown,
Indeed, it had its own.

Adult and grown,
The littlest bird has truly shone.

But today that bird misses the others,
It misses the chatter of poets and prose,
It misses the chords and verses.

Mostly I miss my mum.
It has been a while.
But soon. The nest. I will return.

Empty Together – *Written together*

Two crystal glasses,
Intricately designed,
Exquisite, shinning, beautiful
Empty inside.

Should they be filled,
Brimming, overflowing
coloured with...
red, white, rose, champagne,
Bubbles fighting with each other to get to the brim,
Joyful, frivolous, carefree.

What happened?

The stealth of emptiness crept in
Slowly, surely, steadily
But why?

Surely it wasn't always like this?
A hollowed out existence.

No. No... I remember

I remember it all
But when did the solidification begin?
When did I turn to glass?

Even if filled with the fullest of flavours...
I'm still empty inside.

But I wasn't always like this? So why?

When once I was as light as air,
Floating, dancing without a care
Laughter, trust, smiles all around
My life was simple,
uncomplicated,
unbound.

Childhood, youth went by in a blur
"Come back" I cry…
I want you near!
I want the fun, simplicity of it all
The teenage years – I miss so dear.

Life, experience, distrust crept in.
Replacing the smile with a
Grim
Grin!

I gave my heart, to have it upturned
That is when emptiness and solidification started to churn.

Staring at them again and again
Two crystal glasses
Empty...
But refill them, I will
With life again.

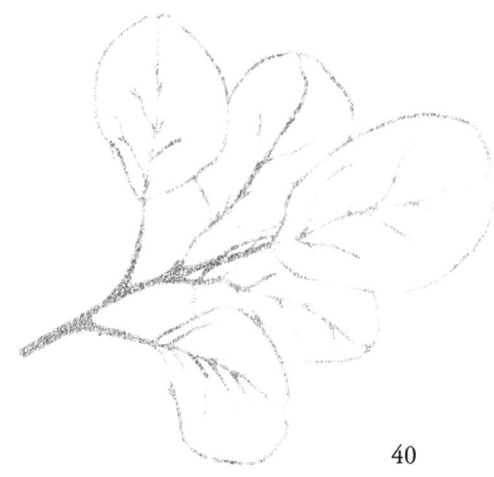

28th May

We are two rocks.
Placed together here by the tide.
For some time now we have been,
By each other's side.

Layered differently,
You are much tougher than I.
Compounded by the millennia,
Are our successes and strides.

The time we have spent,
seems only a day,
Years could pass,
But some things don't change.

Broken with timed winds,
Age weathers us down.
A storm is brewing.
Can you hear the sound?

I am a rock,
Missing you for now.
But when the next surge comes,
I will find my pair somehow.

Seasonal Song

A seasonal song,
Resonating against the walls,
Thumping. Thumping. Thumping.

It picks up where it left,
Ever intense,
I hear... Something

Is it seasonal?
Have I known it all along?
A song it is.

A song is it?
As familiar as a hand.
As a face.
As a land.

I know it.
I know its song,
A chirping of the wilds,
A chirping of the land.
That strange, strange tonal arrangement,
Dissonant and abrupt.
Moment seizing and stealing.

Thank God!
That stolen moment occurred.
That seasonal song...
Well... It was heard.

Slip

I hope time doesn't erase us,
I hope it doesn't erase you
In my mind.

Will it be kind?
Memories lathered for a lifetime,
Please don't forget them like a distant chime.

When does it start?
The fading...
I wonder.

Apart we may be,
But I keep you in my memories.
So I hope they don't fade.
Not entirely,
Not forever,
Not today.

Sand

When I think of you,
A warm smile encumbers my heart.
A laugh soon follows,
As it would, naturally...

A thoughtful soul,
Strangely unsure...
Time... time can make this happen,
It can make us question,
Question our soul.

But for you,
You are so rare,
Unsure but wise,
You are my elder and sometimes,
Sometimes I don't think you see the reflection there.

But I do.
I know who you are.
Clear, is my sight,
You are here.
If I were to say one thing,
That you must hear,
It would be simply,
You are more, than what you think, you appear.

Phase Three — Thought

Preface

The single greatest gift,
Bestowed to us,
Is our thoughts,
They give belonging, a must.

To think and discover,
It is the core,
A privilege we should never,
Never truly ignore.

For the freedom to think,
To chirp our views,
It isn't a given,
History has fought for your cues.

With this right take it wise,
Listen, learn…
Not to everyone should you turn,

Opinions, they come with friendships that go,
Your mind, your thoughts, they are your own.
To share is a choice, one must make alone,

Here are some of our thoughts, shared.

A Star

I saw a star,
Or a star saw me.
As it waved,
I knew, I knew instantly.
A star was waving at me.

It blazed, blistered ever brighter.
Untouchable and not meant for this world,
Only to walk each step once and fade, evermore.

A butterfly flaps its wings,
As it extends fully and catches the breeze stirring,
Uplifted, rising through the sky.

Chasing a star.
Do not waste your life.
But to see one for however long,
To see its steps and for it to see yours.

I saw a star,
And it did see me.

Peace

What a divine scale,
Will it tip either side?
Shall it weigh importance?
Or self-importance...

How absorbed are you?
To deem your life more than mine,
Judging so harshly my actions,
What about yours?

Okay... Okay... Swallow it down,
Have another sip to slow as I drown.

Tighten the lips,
Ready the armour,
There's no war brewing...
Steady... Steady... Steady

What way will it tip?
What is it even weighing?
Why do I care...

You

Who are you?
Who are you?
It is a question asked so often.

Is it a name?
Is that all that I am?
A name,
Easy, I am who my name pertains.

Is it the ever changing appearance?
As we morph and fade with age,
Am I how I look?

Is it simply what we do?
Does this define our entirety?
I am a teacher,
Is that who I am?
Is that all I am?

We are asked many times,
What we want to be?
Who we want to be?

But I still always ask myself...
Who are you?

Bench Thoughts

To sit still for some time,
Time often needing filling,
But to sit still.
It is a magical thing.

As I watch the lives pass before me,
They move with such haste,
They move with such conviction,
Oh, how they move.

The varying degrees of wear and tear on their souls,
I admire those who can't stop,
But I pity them more so.

It is nice,
Truly a pleasure unfathomable to some.
To sit still for some time.

Climb

Sharp glass daggers of pain course through fingers,
Grasping at each hold.
Up. Only up.

Weight seems to be added,
Every second a heavier load.
Up. Only up.

The air thins as the wind howls,
You would think the view would be pleasant.
Up. Only up.

Clinging, dragging myself to the peak,
When will I reach?
When will the climb descend?
Up. Only up.

An Old Soul — *Written together*

From the first moment we met,
To the last moment we get,
It was but an instant,
But I knew, I knew you yet.

The creases on your face,
Etched in by time
Time that had not been done.

An old soul given to me,
Trusted to me,
Sent to me.

And as time stumbled on
You grew into those creases.
Imprinted your essence slowly in pieces.

The very fabric of my being,
absorbed your sweet graces,
encompassing loving embraces.

We chose different paths and never looked back
You came before me as I held back.
Why I wonder did you depart,
So anxious for life
For what I ask?

But now I search, I seek… I surrender,
As the scent is fading, getting fainter
Don't go… Wait – come back,
There is still much to discuss.

It isn't enough.
It will never be enough.

As the sand slips through my fingers,
I clench tighter,
I claw at the grains on the ground
More… is it too much to ask?

An old soul chosen for me,
I accept, I accept willingly.

How was I to know that that soul would be kindred to
my own?
How was I to know a shared spirit would be found?

A longing for a walk down the street to a cafe,
To discuss the sands as they slip away.

Creases much similar to my own,
I long for every conversation, every word, every tone.

The Rabbit – *Written together*

The warmth of the first sun on my weary eyelids
Slowly assists the chill scented breeze in nourishing my
eyes open.
As I blink to focus upon my reality,
I assess my parched tongue and depleted stomach.
Time to gather.

There is a fine layer of dew blanketing the grass
With occasional web traps, sprung at night.
Poor souls.

As I crawl out into this world
I retract at my first contact with the bitter cold of the
morning.
But. I must.
Darting through the dew, galloping across the grass, The
many wonders of the forest floor are passed.

As I lap up the water rehabilitating and revitalising my
morning spirits.
Cccrrackk.
Something's there...

Frozen
I peer cautiously, eyes right... eyes left...
Eyes straight down

Focussed - pinned on the water
Looking for a shadow, a glimmer, an image
Cccrrackk…

Closer… closer… closer it comes
I turn,
Every sense in me heightened.
My smooth hairy coat now agitated – bristling, straight,
upright – attention!

Nose quivering, snot running freely… the smell!
The scent of danger, freedom or perhaps even friendship
Hard to tell
The overwhelming fragrance of …
Ccrrackk…

Still
Still
I must remain still...

Frozen in place I dare not move
My eyes still scanning
Will it come closer?
Will it come...
Come closer...

Crrraackkk
I turn, lightning, and spot the spy.
Our eyes lock as we share a moment of wonder.

Neither of us move at first,
Lingering in our lock…
I move forward to get a closer look.

Whooosh…
It left, darting away into the forest abyss…
Maybe we would meet again, maybe.
But what a strange entanglement for us to meet in the first place.

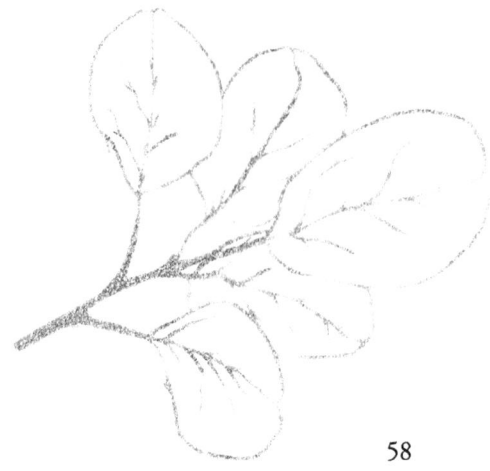

The Hive

What will they think?
The swarm, buzzing with intensity
As they linger... Watching.

Does it matter?
To be part of them... maybe it does?
Their two faced stripes and double standards are ripe
with finality.
Judgement.

But... To be happy
Not the superficial collective happiness.
The kind you receive when in the presence of more.

Your heart is at peace,
Your soul is understood,
Your words, heard.

And your eyes are met
With a pair that can strip past the charade,
Seeing what lies beneath the shallows.
Yes... I think... It could be worth it.
But what will they think?

Healing

There is a time,
Between the first beat of the sun's rays,
And the dew weighted grass it warms,
Where I live.

A place where the mixture of realms align,
Between reality and not.
A place where you are heightened,
Your feelings, thoughts, emotions
All pondered upon between the rays of ever growing
light.

Yes, I… I live here.
Not always.
I visit from time to time.
When my heart has no other place to feel.
When my mind has no other time to ponder.
When my emotions have no other time to heal.

Sometimes it is worth saying something,
I am never a good judge of that.
So I stay here, where I live.
From time to time.
For a little while.

Jimbocho

Listless logic of knowledge from far off lands meet here.
To frolic on fresh blooms
To fertilise the unseen seeds.

From Perth to Perth and everything in between,
From the depth of the core to the fringe of the universe.
This is where the possibilities of our dreams meet.

The infinite realm of meaning and life,
Taking form through timeless words.
The pristine, tranquil trance you may find yourself in.
Don't fear it, you are not alone.

Here… Where?
Everyone and everything is somewhere else.
But you.
You are here.

Great Expectations

We begin. Warm, unaware and loved.
Hopefully loved.
On wings of forward falcons, we fly through time.
Unaware of its fickle nature and how little we truly possess.

Ripples distress us causing eruptions, pyroclastic flows escape through our eyes,
As we grow and can only see the present.
Trapped in the illusion of what we are now...

... Tomorrow, the day after, the year after, the decade after
How quickly the falcon pulls,
How quickly our memory fades to distant ripples.

A firefly lands, unassuming, small, on your hand.
It peers into your soul and extracts a moment.
Fleeting in its presence but permanent in your mind.
Dragging you back, willingly or not, it tugs and throws you to the past.
The past, when present, was not all you had aspired.
When looking back it is more than you could have ever desired.

Trapped in the present and our expectations are such. But through the past we see our great expectations are never truly lost.

Pod

What a pod we are,
Two souls intertwined.
One destined to fly,
The other to merely be bound.

It is the belief,
The arrogance of self,
To think you soar above
When you really are one of the crowd.

This self-perception,
Fostered by liars masked,
Perfection is an illusion,
Why must we be told we are such.

Honesty is a lie now,
It spits venom on our souls,
No one loves honesty,
Too many parents protect from this foretold.

Dreams

As the moon said good night,
To the stars and the sky,
Our dreams for the next day,
As the sun came with its shine.

New hope, new meaning.
The warmth may bring.
Night time,
That is where our dreams begin.

What can be fathomed,
Narrow or wide.
Is only limited by the length in time.

For that is meaning,
As meaning may be.
We are limited by the time,
By the moon,
By the sun,
By what we see.

As it Should Be

To speak as one speaks,
It is taught, it is preached.

To walk as one walks,
It is measured, in leaps.

To see as one sees,
It is deep, it is a need.

To be as one is,
It is, as it was, as it will be.

I suppose at the end of the day,
It is embarrassing to admit…
Some people have deathly fears,
Mine seem less legit.

With great praise,
Talent was seen,
But I fear inadequacy…
I fear just blending in.
Not being enough,
In a multitude of ways.
I fear mediocrity,
But am accepting, it may just be my middle name.

And yet I write,
I try to put a pen to this melancholy vein,
Maybe I am just average,
Is that so strange?

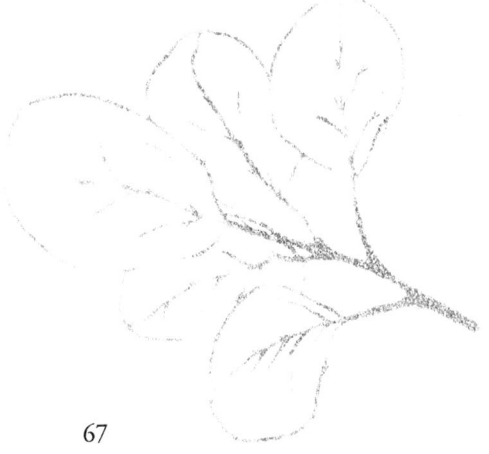

Words

Stolen Words… Lost words… New words
Forbidden words…
Maybe even
Unknown words…

Where do "words" come from?
Our Bones
Brains
Blood… brawn… battlefields
At dawn?

Their power
So strong, meaningful, loving yet hurtful?
Feared by politician
Kings and queens
Friends and foes
All struggle with prose.

Doublespeak, Newspeak,
Synonyms, antonyms
Old English, New English
And then…
Woke.

Words capture our essence our very soul
Our thoughts and feeling
They make us whole.

Yet how they evolve
With us being involved… intertwined, bound, tied to
their meaning
A mystery to solve.

Merville

He swept,
On the side of the road.
As the sun dragged him up,
And kept him there.

Each day with the ebb and flow,
Each day more of him would go.

Time poor, illusive in age,
Eyes of piercing sightlessness.

For sight, vision, and future,
Belong to those of wealth,
Oh, the luxury of purpose.

He remained sweeping,
Everyday.
Until he didn't remain.
I never saw him again…
Not on my way.

The Grey

Strand by strand The Grey comes,
It etches with its scalpel,
Irreversible but timely.
Each carved crevice, precise.

The valleys and creeks,
Eroded over the years,
New favourable formations arise,
The same soulful sight,
With an ever changing image.

The Grey offered me this deal,
To continue on,
In exchange for her art to take form.

Accepted was the deal,
As deals may come as quick as they go,
To live a full life,
With the image as it grows.

Time will tell what the appearance will be,
The Grey, may you be kind to me.

The Voyage

Friend or foe,
The voyage carries all.
It matters not what side of the coin,
Scars will, in tow.

Products of the voyage,
With those that trespass,
Tread lightly if you wish,
The ripples will be less.

Our souls, deserving or not,
Words across ages,
They are stitches into our eventual thoughts.

Our actions are products,
The voyage has allowed,
The manner in which we learn,
Our heart decides.

No matter the vices,
The disputes of the sea,
Both sides of the coin,
They shape who you will be.

Sherry

When the light fades,
And the darkness takes hold,
The spirit uplifts,
From this mortal coil.

The last Sherry sipped,
Sweet, aged, old,
We become the stories,
From mouths told.

As the fly buzzes close to my ear,
Circling ever more, ever near,
Its decaying grip of such I know,
The memories it holds I fear.

For what will the story be?
I don't know, I'm hopefully not near,
My last Sherry sip,
It will be sweet, aged, old and dear.

About the Authors

Sandra Greenwell has been Head of Libraries at international schools in three countries for over 15 years. Besides being a librarian, she is also a senior schoolteacher. Sandra's experience spans from higher education to specialist libraries. Given her background, it is not surprising that Sandra is an avid reader. One of her favourite books is Little Women, but her scope in reading extends to all genres. She loves reading free verse poetry and occasionally dabbles in writing a poem or two and sharing them with her daughter, Cassandra.

Cassandra Greenwell is a senior school Humanities, Social Sciences, and soccer specialist teacher in Western Australia. She grew up attending a range of schools in different countries. Cassandra has always loved playing sports, in particular soccer. However, it wasn't until senior school when she developed a love of poetry and literature. She has fond memories of sitting in Le Delice Café with her mother, Sandra, analyzing poetry and discussing various authors.

Printed in the USA
CPSIA information can be obtained
at www.ICGtesting.com
LVHW060819301023
762334LV00012B/158

9 781960 810052